Google Nexus 7 User's Manual Tablet Guide Book with Tips & Tricks

By Shelby Johnson

Disclaimer:

This eBook is an unofficial guide for using the Google Nexus 7 and is not meant to replace any official documentation that came with the device. The information in this guide is meant as recommendations and suggestions, but the author bears no responsibility for any issues arising from improper use of the Nexus. The owner of the device is responsible for taking all necessary precautions and measures with their tablet.

Google Nexus 7, Google, and Nexus are trademarks of Google or its affiliates. All other trademarks are the property of their respective owners. The author and publishers of this book are not associated with any product or vendor mentioned in this book. Any Google Nexus 7 screenshots are meant for educational purposes only.

Table of Contents

Introduction (What is the Nexus 7) 6

What's in the Box? 7

Setting Up and Using your Nexus 7 8

Choosing a Language 8

Setting up Wi-Fi Network 8

Setting up Email 10

Setting up Facebook and Twitter 12

Setting up Calendar 12

Choosing Location Services 14

Organizing Home Screen 14

Nexus 7 Settings 18

Security Settings 19

Notifications and Settings 19

Device Settings 21

Wireless Settings 22

Nexus 7 Features 24

Daydream 24

Google Play 25

Shop on Google Play 26

Google Now 26

Gesture Typing 27

Movies and Music on Nexus 7 28

Enjoying Music on Nexus 7 28

Watching Movies on Nexus 7 29

Nexus 7 How-To Tips and Tricks 32

How to Use Google Keyboard 32

How to Customize the Lock Screen 33

How to Use Face Unlock 33

How to Share with Android Beam 33

How to Transfer Files 34

How to Take a Screenshot 35

How to use Voice to Text 36

How to Manage Downloads 37

How Maximize Battery Life 38

How to Connect to Keyboards and other Devices 38

How to Convert iTunes media for Nexus 7 39

How to Use Amazon AppStore on Nexus 7 39

Nexus 7 Troubleshooting 41

How to Fix 'Dead' Nexus 7 after LED Blinking 41

How to Reboot to Safe Mode 41

How to Fix an App 42

How to Reset to Factory Settings 42

How to Fix GPS 43

What to do When Device Randomly Reboots 43

How to Fix Flickering Touch Screen 44

How to Fix Touch Sensitivity and Typing Issues 45

25 Great Nexus 7 Apps 47

Pulse News by LinkedIn 47

OneNote 48

Google Drive 48

OfficeSuite 6 Pro 48

Pocket 49

Skype 49

Dropbox 49

iMDB 50

Stitcher 50

Facebook, Twitter, Pinterest & Google+ 50

Mint 51

AirCalc 51

Kindle 51

Free Calls with magicJack 52

Dashlane Password Manager 52

Flipboard: The Content Aggregator 52

Instagram 53

Tweetcaster 53

Hulu Plus (Free & Paid Subscriptions) 54

Netflix (Free & Paid Subscriptions) 55

Pandora (Free & Paid Subscription) 55

Spotify (Free & Paid Subscription) 56

Goodreads App 57

Urbanspoon by Wanderspot 58

Allrecipes.com Dinner Spinner for Android by
    Allrecipes.com 59

Dictionary.com Dictionary and Thesaurus by
    Dictionary.com 60

Fandango Movies - Times & Tickets by Fandango, Inc.
    60

Banking (Credit Card) App 61

10 Great Nexus 7 Games 62

Candy Crush Saga 62

Dungeon Hunter 4 63

Triple Town 63

Words with Friends 64

100 Floors 64

Beastie Bay 65

Can You Escape 2? 65

Gyro 66

Heroes of Order and Chaos 66

Real Soccer 2013 67

Nexus 7 Accessories 68

Case 68

Stylus 68

Screen Protector 69

External Power Chargers 69

WiFi Media Drives 70

Google Chromecast 70

Bluetooth Speakers & Headphones 71

Docking Station from ASUS 71

Conclusion 72

Resources 73

More Books by Shelby Johnson 74

Introduction (What is the Nexus 7)

The Google Nexus 7 is a uniquely priced Android 4.3 Jelly Bean operating platform tablet that brings mobile device users the trusted Google name for an affordable Android tablet that rivals the competition. The Nexus 7 delivers a clean and simple touch screen operation combined with the lightweight-yet-durable construction that weighs in at a meager .64 pounds.

With its ultimate portability and easy to use functionality, the nine hours of video playback, or ten hours of web browsing or e-reading battery life only adds to the allure of this small-but-mighty tablet. The quad-core, Qualcomm Snapdragon S4 processor and 2GB of RAM ensures that everything runs quickly and smoothly, so there is never any delay in your entertainment. Speaking of entertainment, the full 7" scratch-resistant Corning glass screen displays stunning graphics at 1080p HD IPS.

With a 1.2-megapixel front-facing, fixed focus camera and a five-megapixel rear-facing, auto focus camera, you will never miss a minute of action around you, even when you are on the go. Consumers have the option of a WI-FI enable tablet with 16GB of internal storage for the low price of $229; WI-FI enabled 32GB of internal storage for $269; or the latest edition Wi-Fi, LTE, HSPA+ 32GB of internal storage option for $349. Some retailers have even offered deals above and beyond these standard prices.

What's in the Box?

As with everything Google does, simplicity reigns supreme. The Google Nexus 7 box contains the following:

- Google Nexus 7 Tablet
- microUSB Cable
- Wall Charger
- Quick Start Guide
- Product Safety & Warranty Guide

As you'll notice, there isn't any official instruction guide included with the device to help with concepts beyond those in the quick start guide. This guide book serves to provide more help for those looking to get more out of their tablet in a condensed-yet-helpful manual. So let's get started with setting up this innovative device and take advantage of what it has to offer!

Setting Up and Using your Nexus 7

When you turn your Google Nexus 7 on, the first thing you will notice is the intuitive setup options. Videos will walk you through the process, and allow you to fully explore your new device so you get the most from its use.

Choosing a Language

When the device is activated, the very first thing you will do is pick the language you would like displayed.

Setting up Wi-Fi Network

To get any further in the setup process, a WI-FI connection is required. The device will detect the networks near you, and it will be up to you to supply a password for a secure network to be accessed. Once you have connected, you can proceed with the setup process. Keep in mind, you'll need to repeat this process if you're at a hotel, public area, the office, or friend's place with WI-FI.

Select Wi-Fi

NETGEAR-JARK 2 N
Secured with WPA/WPA2 (WPS available)

belkin.390
Secured with WPA2 (WPS available)

belkin.390.5GHz
Secured with WPA2 (WPS available)

ATT5950
Secured with WPA2

belkin.390.guests
WPS available

Brisco
Secured with WPA/WPA2 (WPS available)

ATT4267
Secured with WPA2

ATT809
Secured with WPA/WPA2 (WPS available)

vroom19

$+$ Other network...

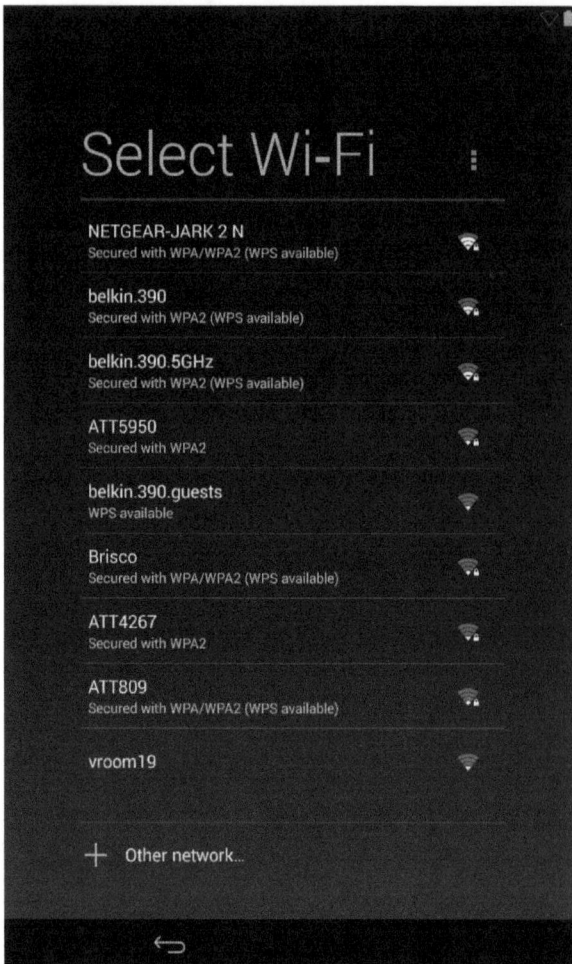

The device will ask you for your Google username and password. If you do not have one of the following accounts, you will need to create an account with the technical giant, and there is no time like the present to do so. You are able to skip this setup segment, but you are going to need a Google account to properly access Google Play later, or operate the device optimally, so there is really no need to skip it. You can head over to Gmail.com and create a free Google email account to do this.

If you have one of the following accounts, use that same username and password to move forward when prompted for your Google account information:

- Gmail
- YouTube
- Google Apps
- AdWords
- Any other Google product

Setting up Email

If you have Gmail, and use that account to sign into your device, it will automatically sync your email, contacts, calendars and events as well as any other data that is associated with your Google account.

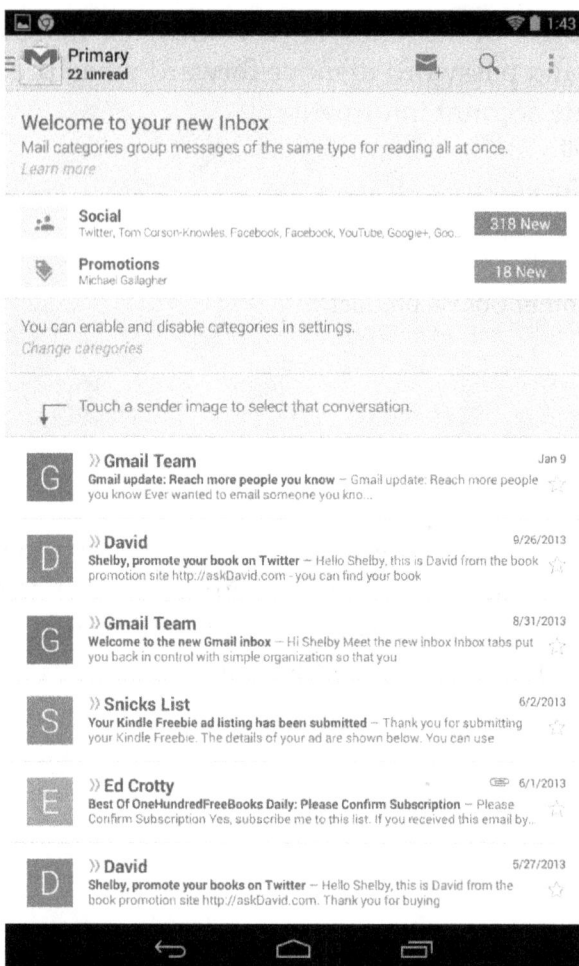

If you have a different email provider, such as Yahoo! AOL or otherwise, simply tap the email app icon, and follow the instructions provided. It will ask you for your email address and password before setting up the account on your device. You can set up as many email accounts as you would like using this method. This makes for a great way to keep track of all your emails at once.

Setting up Facebook and Twitter

In order to access all of your favorite social networks, locate the "Settings" app and tap it to display differing categories. Facebook, Google+, Skype and Twitter are all available. Pick one at a time and set up your account by tapping on the network and entering your username and password for that specific account. Add each network you would like to see updated on your Nexus 7, so you can stay in close contact with friends and family effortlessly.

Setting up Calendar

If you are a fully functioning Googler and already operate your calendar through Gmail, it will automatically sync with your device, so you really do not have to set up an additional calendar. However, should you need to set up dates, meetings, or even add birthdays to the device's calendar, all you have to do is tap on the "Calendar" icon, pick the day of the event, tap "Add New Event," add a category to the event, type the name, location, time and duration of the event and tap "Save."

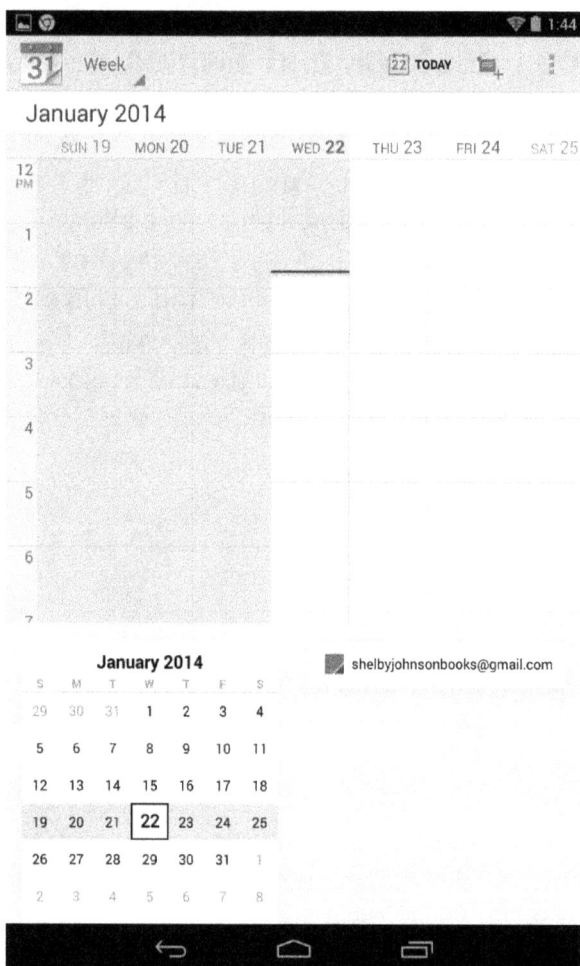

You may also set up a reoccurring event, should you need a reminder each day to take medication or check a stock price!

Choosing Location Services

You will be prompted during setup to enable location services, and it would behoove you to do so. Simply check both boxes, so your device knows where you are – even when you are traveling – so it can provide the best services available for your current existence. This could include navigating you through traffic, providing location information (for the weather forecast, nearest movie theaters or restaurants, perhaps), and to keep you on track with all of your technological needs – like the time zone change where applicable.

Organizing Home Screen

Each Nexus 7 user has the opportunity to set up their home screen as they see fit, providing a truly unique experience for each user.

Simply swipe left to right on the device to view any of the six existing home screens. Although the device comes with a number of widgets already on the screens, you can move or remove them to get the organizational variety you prefer.

To move the icons, simply place your finger over the app's icon and hold it. Once it has been mobilized, simply drag the icon to its – or your – preferred location. This allows you to keep all of your like apps on the same screen, should you so desire. To remove the app altogether, hold the icon until it is mobilized and hit the "X" that appears next to it. You will be asked if are sure you want to delete the app, at which point you can answer as you see fit.

There are literally millions of apps available through Google Play, so you can get new ones, or any old ones back later if you removed them accidentally. You can find some great recommended apps to download in a later section in this manual.

At the bottom of your home screen there is a section that is ever-visible, called the "dock." It will come prearranged with five icons within it, but you can organize it as you see fit with up to six apps.

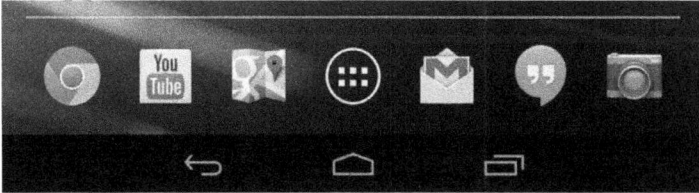

To remove existing apps from the "dock" area, simply drag it using the previous method, and add the replacement app into the area by dragging it directly into the space. You can change these as you see fit, and become more acquainted with the apps you love most, or simply the ones you use the most. For example, you may want Facebook or the Stocks icon readily available.

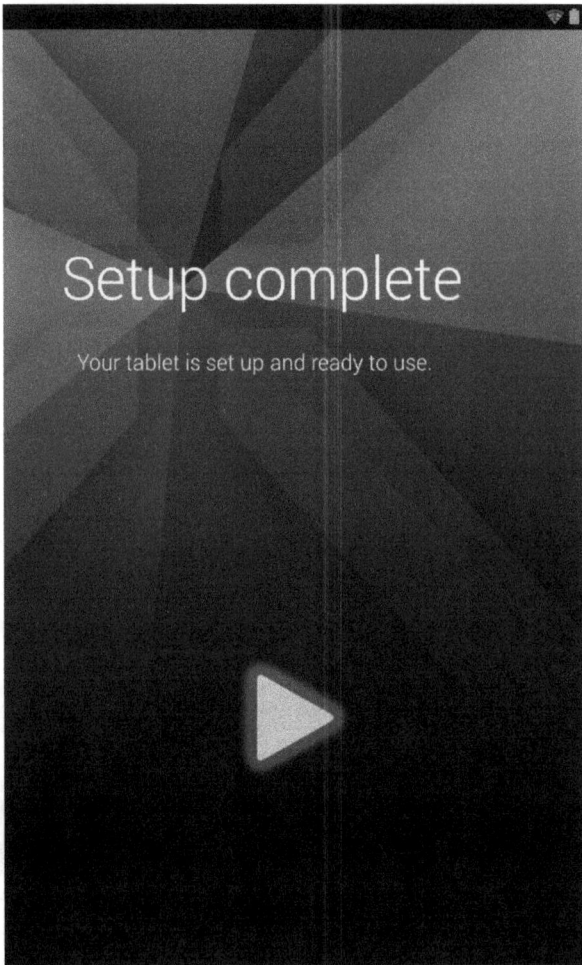

Setup complete

Your tablet is set up and ready to use.

With that, your tablet has now been set up with the basics and you're ready to use your device. Now, let's look more in depth at the settings you'll be able to adjust to optimize your experience.

Nexus 7 Settings

There are a number of settings options on the Nexus 7, and all of them can provide exceptional functionality, as long as you are using them correctly. Some may even help with troubleshooting in the future, should any issues arise.

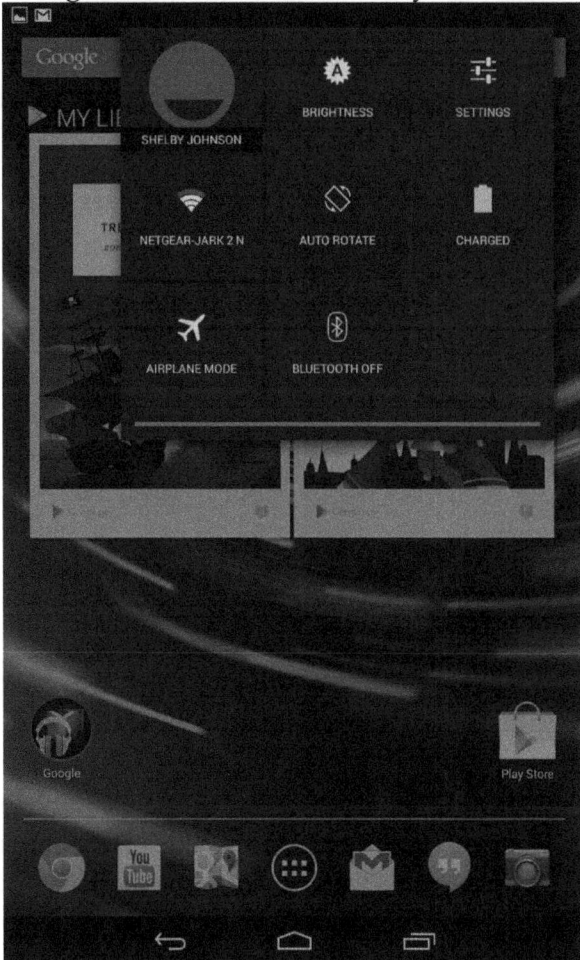

Security Settings

You are going to want to keep you device secure, even if it is from tiny little fingers in your own home, or if you have inadvertently left your Nexus 7 at a coffee shop! Here's how to keep things safe.

To lock your screen, so not just anyone can access your device, follow these steps:

1. Drag down the top right-hand corner of the screen and press Settings.
2. Find the Security option and tap on it.
3. Tap on Screen lock.
4. Choose your locking method: Pattern, PIN, Password or Face Unlock (showing your face to the camera).

You will have to provide this security access clearance each time you want to use your device, so make sure it is something you will remember. It's a wise idea to keep your tablet secure in the event your device is stolen, since it may have lots of personal data and files stored on it.

Notifications and Settings

The Nexus 7 comes with notification signals where a light flashes slowly when the tablet receives new e-mail, a social networking update, or other similar updates. These notifications can include a chime or sound alert as well, so you know when things are happening in real time. You can adjust your notifications, say if you want to know when you get emails, but not necessarily a Facebook notification alert. Or you may be using the tablet somewhere where you need to keep things quiet.

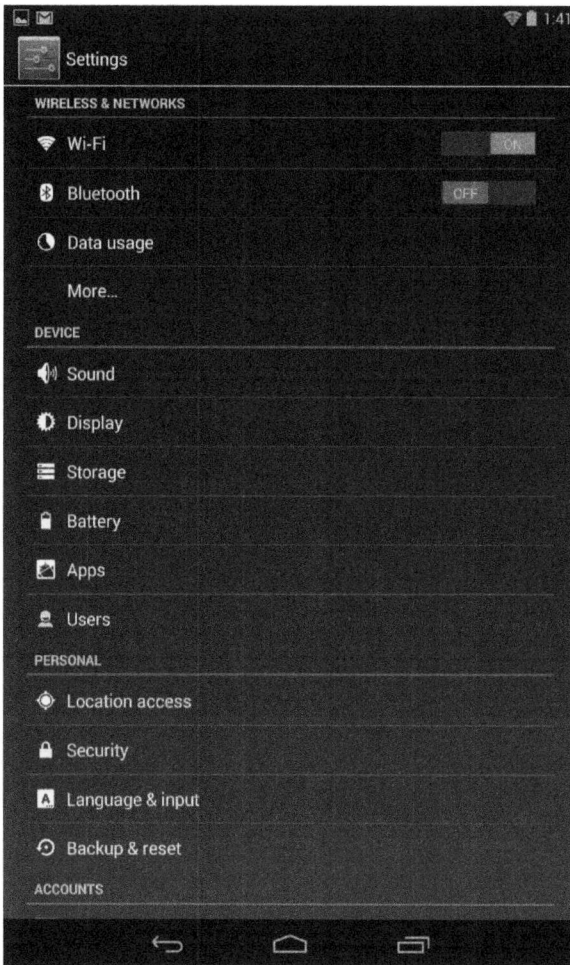

When a notification arrives, its icon appears at the top of the screen. Pending notifications are located on the left, upper-hand side of the screen. Your WI-FI signal and battery strength notifications are located on the upper right-hand side of the screen.

To change your alerts, simply:

- Drag down the top right-hand corner of the screen and press Settings.

To change signal tones, go to Settings > Device > Sound and touch the one you want:

- Volumes sets the master volume separately for music, ringtones & notifications, and alarms. You can still use the physical volume control on the phone to raise or lower volume of whatever sound is currently playing.
- Default notification announces the arrival of notifications unless you specify a different sound in an individual app.
- Touch sounds controls the sounds you hear when you touch buttons, icons, and more.

Device Settings

There are a plethora of device settings that are completely within the user's control, allowing you to setup your tablet exactly the way you want it. Instructions for everything from extending your battery life to printing from your device are included in the Nexus 7 features section listed below.

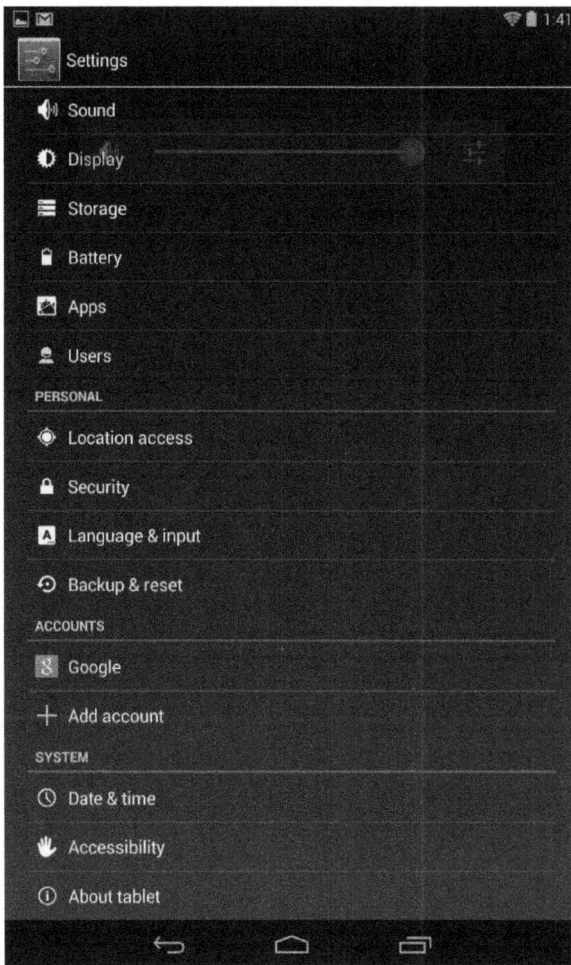

Wireless Settings

Using your device wirelessly is one of the joys of owning a
Nexus 7. No matter where you are, there is a setting that will
accommodate your needs.

To connect to WI-FI:

In your device's Settings menu, touch Wireless & networks >
WI-FI.

1. Slide the WI-FI switch to the On position.
2. The device scans for WI-FI networks. To connect, touch a network
    name.
    *   Secured networks display a lock icon and may ask for security
        details.
    *   Your device will remember the network, along with security
        details, and connect automatically when in range.
    *   To change network settings, touch & hold the network name.

If you need to switch the device to Airplane Mode for travel
purposes, or locate a Virtual Private Network (VPN), you
have access to each of these options in the same place you
found the WI-FI network: Settings > Wireless & networks >
More.

*   Airplane Mode: Select this option to turn off all data transmission
    from the device.
*   VPN: Touch to adjust settings for accessing a secure local network
    from outside that network.
*   Tethering & portable hotspot. If this setting is available on your
    device, touch to adjust settings that allow you to share your
    device's network connection with a computer or several other
    devices, via USB, WI-FI, or Bluetooth.
*   Mobile networks. If this setting is available on your device, touch
    to adjust settings that control your device's connections with
    mobile data networks.

Nexus 7 Features

The Nexus 7 is full of features that allow you to enjoy an exceptional experience each time you use your device. Music, movies and pictures all come to life with the features available. Let's dive into what you'll find among them.

Daydream

Daydream allows your tablet to display images, colors and more while it is docked or charging. To turn Daydream on complete the follow steps:

1. Go to Settings > Device > Display.
2. Touch Daydream.
3. Slide the switch to On. (Use the same directions to turn it off, by sliding the switch back at any time.)

You can decide what displays during Daydream, and how quickly the mode begins under the same settings. However, to hand pick your options compete the following:

- Clock displays the device's digital or analog clock. You can change the clock style or select the Night mode option by touching the Settings icon next to Clock.
- Colors shows changing colors on the screen.
- Photo Frame presents a slideshow of photos on your device or Google+ account. Touch the Settings icon next to Photo Frame to control what photos are displayed.
- Photo Table scatters photos on your device or Google+ account across your screen. Touch & hold an image to move it around the screen, or swipe it away to hide it. Touch the Settings icon next to Photo Table to control what photos are displayed.

Google Play

Google Play store provides pure entertainment through movies, TV shows, books, magazines, and music. You can shop on Google Play, and use the app to enjoy items you have already purchased at any time. There are many free games, apps and other content there, so not everything will cost you to download. There are some great free games and apps listed towards the end of this guide to add to your tablet's functionality and fun.

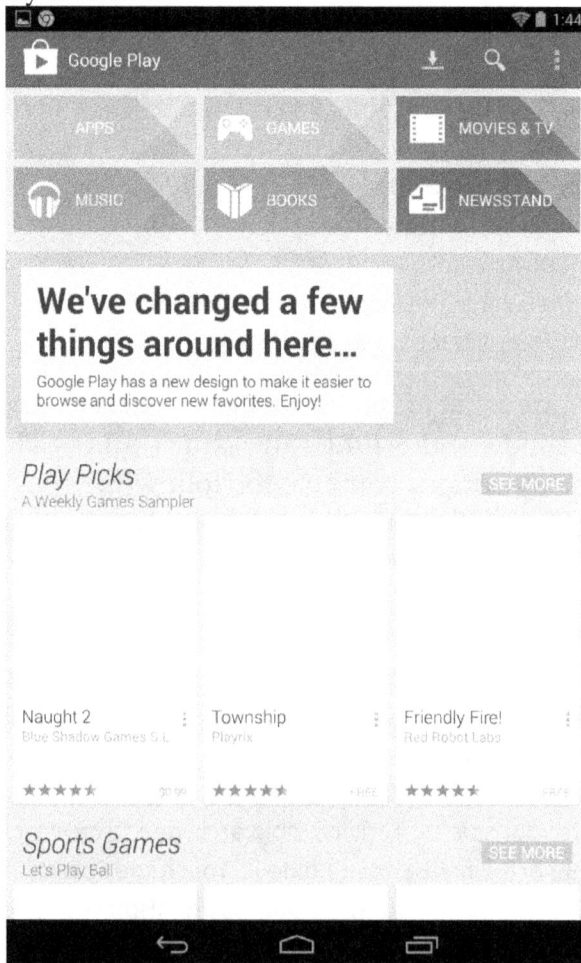

Your library will automatically be saved, and accessible by any Android device as long as you are signed in using your Google account name. This means if you've got an Android phone in addition to your tablet, you should be able to access the apps, games and other content from your Google Play account there.

Shop on Google Play

To open the Google Play Store app, touch the Play Store icon on a Home or All Apps screen. Search for the content you are interested in – even if it is an app that you want to download – and allow Google Play to return suggestions. Once you have found the object of your desire, you can purchase it directly from your tablet using your Google account payment information. If you do not already have a credit card or PayPal account assigned to your Google Play account, you will need to enter the information before the purchase. Remember, some games/apps are free, others are not.

Google Now

The beauty of Google Now is that all of the information the app provides is in real time. You will receive the current weather report before you even get out of bed, current traffic conditions and the score to games played by your favorite teams! To activate these options, and receive a "Card" that contains all of your need-to-know information, simply swipe your finger up from the bottom of any screen.
You can edit your card settings, to receive the current information that is important to you, by tapping go to Menu > Settings > Notifications.

Gesture Typing

Currently Gesture Typing works best in the English language, and may not be available in differing languages yet. If you are currently operating in English, follow these directions to enjoy Gesture Typing:

To input a word using Gesture Typing:

1. Touch the location where you want to type to open the keyboard.
2. Slide your finger slowly across the letters of the word you want to input.
3. Release your finger when the word you want is displayed in the floating preview or in the middle of the suggestion strip. To select one of the words in the suggestion strip, touch it.

If the word you want isn't shown while using Gesture Typing, you can type it out manually. If you gesture a word and want to change it, touch the word to see other choices in the suggestion strip.

Gesture Typing is on by default. To turn it off,

1. Go to Settings > Language & input > Keyboard & input methods > Google Keyboard.
2. Then touch Settings > Gesture typing > Enable gesture typing.

Movies and Music on Nexus 7

The Nexus 7 is a full feature tablet, and no doubt for many owners, watching movies and listening to music will be a regular use of the tablet. Below you can find great information for enjoying your favorite music and movies on the Nexus 7.

Enjoying Music on Nexus 7

If you've got a lot of music that you've purchased online, and/or stored offline, you can definitely use your Nexus 7 to enjoy it. Among my recommended choices for enjoying music on your device are Google Play and Amazon MP3 store. Google Play Music has one of the most user-friendly and sleek interfaces imaginable. It is a true rival for iTunes. The app is automatically installed onto all Google Nexus devices. Therefore, you do not have to worry about having to download this particular application. Because your device is a pure Google product, you are going to benefit the most from utilizing this particular application for your music streaming pleasure. It will give you the most functionality and best results.

Believe it or not, but Amazon has excellent access to music, as well. With Amazon, you can download albums, singles, and playlists. With Amazon, you will be able to purchase music and play it as often as you would like, with any device that has an Amazon application, or access to the Internet. This includes the Google Nexus 7. If you don't have the Amazon MP3 app installed, do so, and enjoy any of the music files you buy at the Amazon MP3 store, right on your device. You can also keep the files stored in your Amazon cloud online, or right on the device for playback on the go.

Unfortunately, you can't use the iTunes Music Store on your device without some serious hacking, which isn't recommended as it could ruin your tablet. Also, some iTunes music files may not necessarily work on the Nexus 7 right away, but you may be able to use conversion programs on a laptop or PC to change your music format so that you can enjoy it on your tablet.

There are some additional music streaming options listed in the recommended apps section in this guide. I would also recommend storing music files in a cloud online to save space on your device, or purchasing a Wi-Fi media drive to allow for more storage and enjoyment of your music collection.

Watching Movies on Nexus 7

There are various ways to enjoy older and newer movies on your device, including Netflix, Hulu, Google Play movies, and VUDU. Some of these services are paid for monthly, although you may be able to enjoy some free content on the standard Hulu. In terms of renting movies, VUDU, Google Play and Amazon are among the top choices.

Redbox and Netflix are among the latest media services out there for your device. Netflix is the clear winner in this category based on their selection of content including classic movies, TV shows and their own exclusive series. If you are looking to stream television and/or movies, and you have a Netflix subscription, you will want to utilize this application for your Nexus 7. The Netflix will also work great for streaming content to specific HDTV's, or those that you use a Google Chromecast device with.

Hulu Plus is a great application on the Nexus 7 for users that enjoy watching a lot of old movies and/or new television series. Hulu Plus does cost money and requires a monthly subscription fee. However, you can utilize a free trial for 30 days to test out whether or not you enjoy the content that Hulu Plus offers. The interface is excellent and is a real pleasure to use on the Nexus' beautiful screen.

Amazon Instant Video and Amazon Prime are two other alternatives for watching streaming content. Amazon Prime members are able to watch many movies free with their yearly subscription. Some movies that were offered for free on there as of this publication included "Marvel's The Avengers," "The Hunger Games," "Skyfall," and "Flight." There are also movies available for rent, which normally cost $4.99 for standard format and $5.99 for hi-definition.

VUDU.com is a service similar to Amazon, which allows viewers to rent and stream movies on their device. This service generally has newer movies available that are available for rental at other outlets such as Redbox. From time to time, they may also have movies available for rent or purchase that are still in theaters or about to be.

HBO Go is yet another way to enjoy content on your device. If you are currently an HBO subscriber through your cable or satellite TV provider, you'll want to see if you can use HBO Go. If you can, consider installing the app on your Nexus 7 to enjoy movies and shows on your device from HBO's generous selection of content.

Nexus 7 How-To Tips and Tricks

There are a number of tips and tricks that accompany this device, and the more you know, the more you can enjoy its overall functionality. Here's some of the best tips and tricks for the tablet.

How to Use Google Keyboard

In an effort to type up a quick email, or enter a search without delay, use the Google Keyboard at any time. Simply open the keyboard by touching anywhere on the screen you would like to type, and the cursor will blink to indicate positioning.
To use other keyboard tools, follow these directions:

1. Move the insertion point: Touch where you want to type.
2. Select Text: Touch & hold or double-tap within the text.
3. Delete text: Touch the "Back" icon to delete selected text or the characters before the cursor.
4. Type capital letters: Touch the Shift key once to switch to capital letters for one letter.

Or touch & hold the Shift key while you type. When you release the key, the lowercase letters reappear.

- Turn caps lock on: Double-tap or touch & hold the Shift key. Touch the Shift key again to return to lowercase.
- Cut, copy, paste: Select the text you want to manipulate. Then touch the Cut, Copy, or Paste button.

How to Customize the Lock Screen

Locking the screen was covered in a previous entry, but the selection chosen can be changed at any time should you prefer to jump between a PIN number or Pattern.

1. Drag down the top right-hand corner of the screen and press Settings.
2. Find the Security option and tap on it.
3. Tap on Screen lock.
4. Choose your locking method: Pattern, PIN, Password or Face Unlock (showing your face to the camera).

How to Use Face Unlock

Face Unlock is an awesome way to lock your tablet, and also the quickest and easiest way to unlocking, simply by holding the tablet in front of you for facial recognition purposes. Here's how: Tap: Settings > Personal > Security > Screen Lock and choose "Face Unlock." The device will capture your image and use it as a security method.

How to Share with Android Beam

Nexus 7 allows you to place your device against another's and "Beam" web pages, videos or images between the two devices. Perfect for sharing content and information, this exciting feature can be accessed effortlessly.
Note: Before you begin, make sure both devices are unlocked, support Near Field Communication (NFC), and have both NFC and Android Beam turned on.

1. Open a screen that contains something you want to share, such as a webpage, YouTube video, or place page in Maps.
2. Move the back of your device toward the back of the other device.
3. When the devices connect, you hear a sound, the image on your screen reduces in size, and you see the message "Touch to beam."
4. Touch your screen anywhere.

Your friend's device displays the transferred content.

How to Transfer Files

Sharing information and files is simple, and only requires a USB port to upload content to a laptop, PC or MAC. You may need to install the additional Android File Transfer program in order to transfer files to MACs. This can be obtained through a simple Google search for "Android File Transfer." To transfer files onto a PC or MAC simply:
1. Connect your device to the USB port on your computer.
2. Copy files back and forth as you would with any other external device.
3. When you finish, eject the device safely before unplugging the USB cable.

Alternate ways of transferring files include the "Android Beam" method mentioned above, Bluetooth, emailing files, and/or uploading them to a Dropbox account with the app mentioned later in this guide.

How to Take a Screenshot

If you would like to capture a moment in time – or would simply like to take a screen shot of directions, a recipe or anything else that interests you – a screenshot is the perfect way to go about it. Taking screenshots is simple on the Nexus 7.

1. Make sure the image you want to capture is displayed on the screen.
2. Press the Power and Volume Down buttons simultaneously.

The image will now save to your photo gallery. You can also automatically share a screenshot using the "share" icon that shows up after you take it as pictured below.

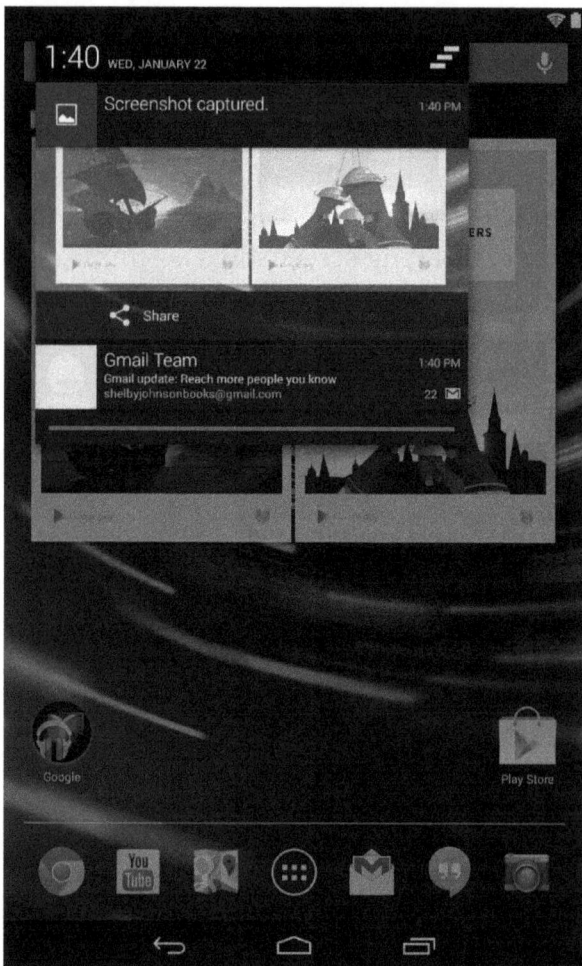

How to use Voice to Text

If you have your hands full, yet still need to get a note jotted down, try the voice to text dictation method that is available to help you remember exactly what you need from the store - or when you have schedule an appointment. This feature is available for speaking words into many areas on the tablet, to make it easier than typing. To activate Voice to Text, simply:

1. Touch a text field, or a location that has already entered in a text field.
2. Touch the Microphone key on the onscreen keyboard.
3. When you see the microphone image, speak what you want to type.

You will have to say things like, "Comma," "Period," or "Exclamation Point" to capture the essence of your message in full. Speak as clearly as possible while enunciating words to make sure it correctly captures what you say. Also, keep in mind some proper names and words may not be instantly recognizable by the device, so these may need to be manually entered.

How to Manage Downloads

Managing downloads can be important to maximize the space on your device. In an effort to keep tabs on what you have downloaded, simply take a look inside from time to time. Start by touching the Downloads icon on the All Apps screen. From the Downloads app:

1. Touch an item to open it.
2. Touch headings for earlier downloads to view them.
3. Check items you want to share. Then touch the Share icon and choose a sharing method from the list.
4. Check items you want to delete. Then touch the Trash icon.
5. At the top of the screen, touch the three horizontal lines to sort your downloads By name, By date modified, or By size.

How Maximize Battery Life

You can extend your battery's life between charges by turning off features that you do not need, or are not currently using. These options will help extend your battery life in a pinch!

1. Turn off Bluetooth. Settings > Wireless & network > Bluetooth
2. Turn down screen brightness. Settings > Display > Screen brightness.
3. Set a shorter Sleep time. Settings > Display > Sleep.

You will be able to see exactly which applications are taking the most battery power by going to Settings > Device > Battery. After assessing the output, you may be able to adjust the settings that are affecting power usage, or stop the app completely. You can also consider finding free or paid Battery Life apps from Google Play to help determine and optimize your device's battery usage.

How to Connect to Keyboards and other Devices

Connecting to a keyboard, mouse or other device is simple and will allow you to expand your tablet's capabilities in no time. Make sure the device you are attempting to pair is Bluetooth-compatible in order for this to properly work. Some items that you may be able to pair with Nexus 7 include Bluetooth keyboards, headsets, media storage drives and other mobile phones or tablets.

To pair and connect a Bluetooth input device to your Nexus 7:

1. Touch Settings > Wireless & Networks > Bluetooth.
2. Make sure Bluetooth is turned on.
3. Touch the name of your device near the top of the screen, so that the text below says "Visible to all nearby Bluetooth devices."

4. Touch Search for devices.
5. When the name or ID of your Bluetooth device appears, touch it and follow the instructions to pair the devices.

How to Convert iTunes media for Nexus 7

You may want to enjoy iTunes media on your device, since not all music and video files play nice on each device. In order to access your iTunes media on your Nexus 7, you are going to need to convert the files to a playable format. This means stripping the files of from the DRM format that iTunes automatically applies to the files.

To convert iTunes media, download any iTunes converter that you find on the Internet. Depending on which computer operating system you have, you should be able to find one that works for your system. A few popular ones are softonic, iTunes converter, and iTunes Music to MP3 Converter. Choose the one that works best for your computer.

How to Use Amazon AppStore on Nexus 7

There may some individuals who prefer using Amazon's AppStore on the Nexus 7 tablet instead of, or in addition to, the Google Play store. Among the benefits of using the Amazon AppStore are that there is a free daily app available, which is normally a paid app. In addition, some find the search and reviews of Amazon's AppStore more helpful.

amazon appstore
FOR ANDROID

Find your favorite apps in the Amazon Appstore.

Including a paid app for free every day. It's easy to get started.

Download the Amazon Appstore

Please keep in mind, this is an option which will involve installing a special file onto your tablet, known as an .apk file. If needed, you can always go through the uninstall steps to remove the app from your device.

To install Amazon Appstore on Nexus 7 complete the following steps:

1. You'll need to allow installation of a third party app on your Nexus 7, to do this go to Settings > Security and then tap on "Unknown sources" to check it off.

2. Tap OK on the warning that pops up, if you are ok with proceeding.

3. Go to install Amazon Appstore area of the site and tap on "Download the Amazon Appstore." You may get another pop-up warning before you can proceed, but tap OK on this.

4. The Amazon AppStore will download onto your tablet. To install it, you can go to your apps, then "Downloads." Tap on the AmazonApps-release.apk.

5. You'll receive a pop-up box which will let you know what the app will have access to on your tablet. Tap on "Next" and then tap "Install" to proceed. If you get a pop-up box from Google, tap on "Accept."

6. The Amazon Appstore will be installed. After a few minutes a new pop-up box comes up, tap "Open" to use the AppStore. You can now sign into your Amazon account.

This newly-installed Amazon AppStore app will be available where the rest of your apps are located for future use, and you can now enjoy the options and selections available from Amazon's app store on your tablet!

Nexus 7 Troubleshooting

As easy as your Nexus 7 device is to use, there may be a time when you just need to reboot or fix a trouble app. Never fear, as troubleshooting is easier than you think. Try these fixes first before you decide to return your device.

How to Fix 'Dead' Nexus 7 after LED Blinking

There have been cases reported online of the Google Nexus 7 going dead, with the only sign of life being its LED lights blinking five times. Should this happen to you, simply charge the device for an hour or more, and turn the device back on. Sometimes this "dead" existence is the result of something draining the battery completely, so it appears as though it will not turn on. Charging it completely, without using the device during that period, is the answer.

How to Reboot to Safe Mode

If you are having trouble with your device, and it is freezing, crashing or delivering errors consistently, the issue could be with a certain app. Rebooting the device in safe mode will help you understand where the issue lies.

1. Ensure your device's screen is on, then press & hold the Power button.

2. Touch & hold the Power off option in the dialog box.
3. Touch OK in the following dialog to start safe mode.

How to Fix an App

If you have an app that is not working properly, there are a couple of steps you can take to fix it, before ultimately contacting the developer if the problem persists.

1. Check to see if there is an update for the app available in the Google Play store.
2. Go to Settings > Apps, select the app in question, and then touch Force stop.
3. Go to Settings > Apps, select the app in question, and then touch Clear cache.
4. Go to Settings > Apps, select the app in question, and then touch Clear data. Caution: Any data saved in this app will be erased.
5. Try uninstalling and reinstalling the app.
6. If you downloaded the app from the Google Play store, try contacting the developer of the app for further assistance.

How to Reset to Factory Settings

If you want to give the Nexus 7 as a gift, or simply sell it to upgrade to a new model, you will want to reset it to its factory settings, so all of your personal information, data, apps and images are removed from its memory. Here's how...

1. Go to Settings > Backup & reset.
2. Touch Factory data reset.
3. Touch Reset tablet.
4. If your tablet is password protected, you'll be prompted to enter your Pattern, PIN, or Password.
5. Touch Erase everything to confirm.

Note: *You'll want to make sure you've backed up all your info and data to another location before performing the above steps.*

How to Fix GPS

The Google Maps is one great way to use the GPS feature and functionality of the Nexus 7. However, there are some users who may find that if they use multiple GPS-based apps, they experience the GPS functionality dropping and not reconnecting. One solution for this is to reboot the device by holding down the power button until it restarts. Make sure to ignore the pop-up box that comes up and allow it to restart. The other unfortunate solution might be limiting use of GPS apps on your Nexus to just one app that uses it. Google Maps is a great one to keep handy for navigation and directions, or you may find there is another GPS app you prefer as your go-to app.

What to do When Device Randomly Reboots

If you experience your tablet randomly rebooting or restarting in the middle of a task, there are several ways to potentially solve this. One solution is to check that your Nexus 7 is updated to the latest Android operating system version. Tap "Settings" and "System Updates" to make sure your system is up to date. If not, tap "Check Now" or "Update" to install the latest Android version.

If your current Android operating system is up to date, the next thing to check is that your apps are updated. The reboot/restart issue may be due to using an app that is conflicting with the operating system. To update your apps, head to the Play Store, tap on "Menu" and then "My apps." Look for an "Update all" option at the top right of the screen to update your apps to the latest versions.

A soft reset is another possible solution. You can do this by holding down your Nexus 7 power button for 30 seconds. Disregard the pop-up options and your device will reboot. The final solutions are a factory reset or taking your device back to the retailer you originally purchased it from. To perform a factory reset, you'll first want to make sure you have saved or backed up all the content you have on your Nexus 7 to somewhere besides the tablet.

Next, tap on your "Menu" button and choose Settings > Backup & reset > Factory data reset > reset tablet. You may be required to enter your password or PIN in order to complete this reset. You'll be prompted to "Erase everything." Once you tap this, your Nexus 7 will reset back to original factory settings and you can start fresh. Again this is a permanent, and usually a last resort for solving problems on the device.

How to Fix Flickering Touch Screen

There have been some Nexus 7 tablet owners who have noticed their screen flickering. This tends to show up on the lower brightness settings, so one workaround is to turn auto-brightness off. You can find this by tapping on Settings gear icon on your tablet, then tap "Display" and tap "Brightness." There you can adjust the current screen display brightness or turn the "Auto Brightness" to off. If you shut this off, make sure you adjust the screen brightness slider to brighter than 40% for optimal viewing.

In the instance that you are continuing to experience a flickering screen issue, it's best to get a replacement tablet from the retailer you originally purchased from. Many users have reported that new replacement tablets they received didn't have the flickering issue.

How to Fix Touch Sensitivity and Typing Issues

Some Nexus 7 owners may notice issues regarding erratic skipping around and multiple touches registering on their screens. It's important to note that this could be an issue related to the screen protector, or possibly a faulty tablet. Another consideration is if you have been using another device that has a different level of sensitivity, you may not be accustomed to the touch sensitivity on the Nexus 7.

A specific app could be causing this issue. A way to diagnose and repair this is by booting your Nexus 7 into safe mode. Do this by holding the power button down, then touch and hold "Power off." Tap on "OK" in the next pop-up box. If you are noticing the tablet works better in safe mode, then it's time to remove apps one-by-one until you determine which is causing the problem.

One app that some users have previously pointed out is the Currents app which is preinstalled on the tablet. Tap on this app icon (a bluish circle) and then tap the 3 small squares shown in the upper right-hand corner of the screen. Tap on "Settings" and make sure to uncheck "Enable background sync," as this may potentially solve the touch sensitivity or erratic touch issue.

The Yet Another MultiTouch Test app is a free app which helps test out the touch on your screen. If you are continuing to see issues when using this app, it's probably time to send the tablet in for a replacement if it still qualifies for one.

25 Great Nexus 7 Apps

With literally millions of apps available on the Nexus 7, as an Android device, it may take a while for you to realize which ones are important to you, and which ones you can absolutely live without. To get you headed in the right direction, try some of these on for size! Most are free and offer pro upgrade versions for a price.

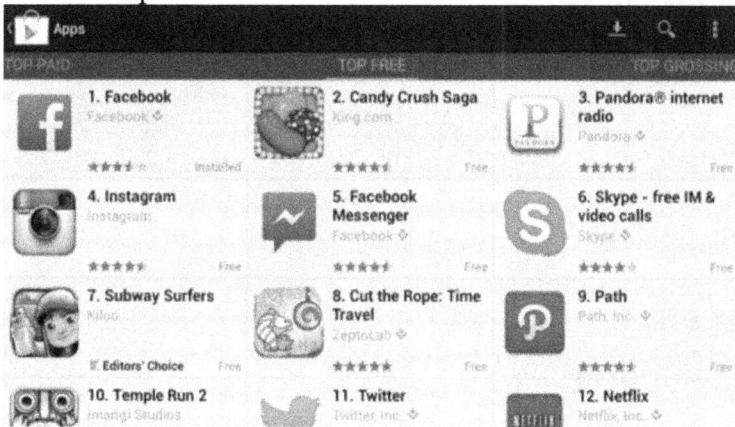

Pulse News by LinkedIn

Not only can you get all of your news in one place, this exceptionally designed app from LinkedIn delivers a breathtaking format that allows you to use its grid design to only read the things that interest you. You can easily share the headlines directly from the home page, so everyone is up to speed on what interests you.

OneNote

Nexus 7 does not come equipped with a note-taking device, so downloading OneNote will keep your to-do lists, grocery reminders and last second jots of information organized and readily available when you need them.

Google Drive

Download, document, back-up and share information using Google Drive's virtual cloud that also operates as Google Docs. You can create spreadsheets, documents and media files and share them effortlessly by providing your audience with a simple link.

OfficeSuite 6 Pro

If you use your Nexus 7 for work, chances are you may need to edit Microsoft documents as a result, and OfficeSuite 6 Pro will give you that latitude turning your tablet into a mainframe computer at home or on the go. There have been free and paid versions of this app available, with the upgraded version offering much more robust features and functionality.

Pocket

If you are an avid online article reader, Pocket allows you to save those pages for future use – much like a DVR will for your TV shows and movies at home. You can also control the font size of the articles, color schemes and even has computer generated speech capabilities so the device will read to you!

Skype

Devices such as the iPad use the popular Facetime app, which unfortunately Google does not have. There is no reason why you cannot stay in touch with loved ones at all times, is there? Not when you have Skype downloaded to your device! Simply ring up another and talk or chat for hours without spending a single dime. There are some aspects of Skype that will require payment, but for the most part, this is a popular free voice/video conference app to use.

Dropbox

Share files, images, movies and data with friends, coworkers, and family members, or allow them to share with you effortlessly by dropping the files they want you to see into your Dropbox. This is a perfect way to share information, without clogging up your memory, or your email space. It can also help you to upload files from your tablet, in the event it should ever crash, or if you need to perform a factory reset. Upload important files, photos, music and other content to Dropbox, and then access it from the internet at the Dropbox.com website via your account.

iMDB

There is always going to be a time when you are watching a movie and think "Oh my gosh! Is that the girl from Back to the Future?" Well, maybe not something that specific, but you get the idea. iMDB allows you to look up an actor or actress, movie title, director – you name it – and receive their entire dossier as a result. This is considered one of the top apps to get for your device, and especially if you're a fan of movies.

Stitcher

Stitcher Radio allows you to listen to talk radio and podcasts by pooling sources from around the world, including BBC, CNN and NPR. Certainly worth checking out and using as part of your overall content options on the tablet.

Facebook, Twitter, Pinterest & Google+

No matter which social media outlets you enjoy best, adding their app to your Nexus 7 is a genius way to pull up the happenings of others – or to add your own – with a single tap of the app's icon. Download only the ones you use now, or become a member in a new area of popularity, like Instagram! Some of these may already be built into your device, while others you'll want to make sure you have to stay updated with the latest social media. Several of the apps may also have ways to integrate with each other, so you'll likely see those in the settings areas on the specific apps.

Mint

If you want to start budgeting your money efficiently, Mint has you covered. You can enter your expenses, deposits, savings and numerous classifications of all things financial. In return, the app will provide you with stellar graphics of your incoming wages and outgoing expenditures so you can see exactly where your cash is coming and going.

AirCalc

You can never have access to a calculator fast enough; especially when you are trying to add up a few things on a certain page – and going back and forth becomes confusing. The AirCalc allows you to overlay a calculator directly into the app or page you are currently on, so there is no more back and forth.

Kindle

You do not have to actually own a Kindle e-reader to enjoy its functionality! With the Kindle app for Android, you can manage all of your favorite eBooks from the palm of your hand, and read to your heart's desire wherever you are, at any time. You can manage your library, stop and start where you left off and even highlight passages just as you would with an actual Kindle device. The great part of this is all of the eBooks you've purchased online at Amazon are stored in your "cloud" area online, so you can access them and read them on the Nexus 7.

Free Calls with magicJack

The free Magic Jack app allows you to make free calls to US and Canadian phone numbers – or to any Magic Jack number in the world. This app does not require a phone plan or purchased minutes. It is completely free, with only WI-FI necessary for use! A great way to save on your monthly cell phone minutes for your plan!

Dashlane Password Manager

Dashlane is a virtual vault that allows you to import your passwords and manage them without having to remember each one, for every site you visit, bank, shop or logon to for any reason. Simply download the app, and import all of your passwords into the secure system. You will never have to type your login information again, and you will be the first one notified in case of a security breach. This app is completely free, and incredibly helpful.

Flipboard: The Content Aggregator

Flipboard is an awesome actionable app that collects content from social media, news and information sites and presents them in magazine format on your device. Users can then "flip" through their social-networking feeds and a host of other websites that partner with the company as well. You can pick and choose what appears on your Flipboard, and easily flip through the content as you see fit anywhere, at any time. This app is completely free.

Instagram

Instagram is an awesome app that is part social network, part photo sharing and part video sharing services that connect you with others who use the same service. You can take pictures using the signature Instagram square shape, and apply 16 different filters as you see fit including Sepia tones, black and white and Lomo-Fi.
The app allows you to connect to your Facebook, Twitter, Tumblr or Flicker accounts effortlessly so you can share your photos or short videos with your social media followers. Likewise, Instagram itself is a social media site where other members can comment on your photos, and you can comment on theirs. This app is completely free.

Tweetcaster

Tweetcaster is a Twitter app that allows you to control your feed, while viewing it in a much more user friendly way than the Twitter app does alone. With the great landscape view you can search based on the media you are looking for, whether it is pictures, videos or hashtags.
This app also gives you the freedom of employing "Zip It" which allows you to silence the individuals you follow when they are talking about topics you are simply sick of. Say, politics or music. Without unfollowing them altogether, you can mute hashtag focused comments, so you do not have to see 300 posts about the current American Idol cast, if you don't want to that is. The app is free, but also comes with banner ads that you will have to live with unless you want to pay $4.99 for the professional version.

Hulu Plus (Free & Paid Subscriptions)

The Hulu Plus app gives you the freedom to watch current television episodes of all your favorite sitcoms, dramas or even sci-fi programs, while adding the luxury of catching up on classic programming like *Arrested Development*. The streaming media app basically allows for binge watching in any capacity, whether it is season one of *Battlestar Galactica* that suits your fancy, recent episodes of pro wrestling TV shows, or the previous season of *Community*.

You can also watch children's programming on demand, and as often as you would like. So if your child cannot go a day without watching his or her favorite episode of SpongeBob, you will never have to worry about finding it at a moment's notice.

You can also enjoy movies, webisodes and trailers all with the tap of the app's icon. You can sign up for free, but for only 30 days. The subscription service itself is $7.99 per month to enjoy unlimited access to television episodes, videos and movies. This app is especially helpful to have if you also have the Google Chromecast streaming media device, which is mentioned later in the accessories section of this guide.

Netflix (Free & Paid Subscriptions)

If Hulu Plus had a rival, Netflix would be it. For the same monthly price of $7.99, and the same free 30 days of programming offered when you sign up for an account, users can enjoy movies, television programming, trailers and webisodes you would on Hulu Plus. Viewing is unlimited, and you can even rate and review what you watched for others to read. Netflix also offers its very own original programming, which has received rave reviews – mostly in the form of Kevin Spacey's drama "House of Cards" and the fourth season of *Arrested Development* that was released exclusively through Netflix. This is yet another app that is compatible with the Google Chromecast accessory for your television.

Pandora (Free & Paid Subscription)

Pandora Radio is a musical app that allows the user to input song titles or artists, and the "station" plays music matching those requests, while spinning additional tunes that are relative and similar to those entries. For instance, if the user enters "Nirvana" as a search artist, it will also play artists like Pearl Jam and Alice in Chains.

The user can provide negative or positive feedback to each song, allowing Pandora to hone the user's musical preferences more closely. Users are offered the option to purchase songs or entire albums during their listening experience, but are not required to do so to enjoy the music. There are two subscription options available with this app. One is the free service, which is supplied through advertisements, or another is the fee-based subscription that allows music to play without ads. The Pandora library is comprised of 800,000 tracks, from over 80,000 artists. There is no cost to download the app itself and begin enjoying all sorts of music through your device.

Spotify (Free & Paid Subscription)

The Spotify app allows users to stream music directly from their tablet while searching for particular musical interests using song titles, artists, album title, record label or genre. Users must have a Facebook account to use Spotify, and are required to login to the service using that account to enjoy the music. Upon initiation of a Spotify account, a free six month subscription is enacted and supplies the user with unlimited usability during that time. At the close of that trial period, song play is limited to ten hours per month – in two and one half hour increments per week – without a subscription. During those ten hours the listener is subjected to advertisements as a way to pay for the service. An unlimited listening subscription is available, allowing users access to music whenever they choose, without ads. A premium service is also available that allows the music to stream at a higher bit rate, and also provides offline access to music. The app is free to download to your Google Nexus 7.

Goodreads App

Goodreads provides readers of all ages with access to book reviews, and the online reading community by delivering the power of social media and interactivity to the Kindle, while intermingling the popularity of the two with the bookworm's penchant for, well, good reads. The app allows individuals to add books to the virtual bookshelf in an effort to share them with the over ten million members of the Goodreads community. With over 12 million books to choose from – with thousands of them falling under public domain (read: free!) – including exceptional reviews and the ability to share the books info in its entirety through Pinterest, Facebook, Twitter, text message or email. What's more is the app includes a barcode scanner, so its user can simply scan the ISBN from any book – in a home, bookstore or doctor's office – and add it to their "to-read" list. Friends, family members and strangers can all rate and review the books they have read, join online book clubs, and even find a literary engagement such as a book signing in their own cities. Never buy another book again, without getting the world's input first.

Urbanspoon by Wanderspot

Urbanspoon not only provides a fun way to make a decision about where to eat, thanks to its restaurant slot machine, where users shake their devices to reveal a digital pick for any meal, but it provides informative, up-to-date information to insure that the restaurant you choose is still operating from the given location. Whether users are looking for a specific type of food – Italian, Moroccan, Mexican and the like – or are simply entertaining their four-star palette, this app divides and conquers the results to its users' requests to provide exact results with each use. The popularity and pricing of restaurants is just as easy to find, and it allows you to check the table availability and even make reservations directly from the app. Users can read reviews from other patrons, while posting their own after enjoying a meal, location or even the ambience. Once users choose a restaurant, they can map it through the app, and get step by step instructions on how to get there. It is fun, easy and a fantastic tool for travelers.

Allrecipes.com Dinner Spinner for Android by Allrecipes.com

Instead of wasting time in front of the refrigerator, trying to make heads or tails of the ingredients that fall within it, Allrecipes.com has created an app for everyone to get dinner on the table, without giving it a second thought. Users can type in ingredients, whether it is asparagus or couscous; dish types, including appetizers, main and desserts; and even cook times for those who have all night, or need something pulled together quickly. The actual "spinner" comes into play when users shake their mobile device to unveil unique meal ideas, which will inspire the chef in everyone – even the most novice kitchen dweller. Lastly, users can search by dietary restrictions, including low-fat, vegetarian, vegan, low sodium, and gluten free, while receiving nutritional information. The app also allows its users to collect recipes, and share them with others through Facebook, Twitter and email.

Dictionary.com Dictionary and Thesaurus by Dictionary.com

The preeminent source for all things word-related, including the correct spelling, definitions, antonyms, synonyms, phonetic and audio pronunciations come to life with the use of this brilliant app. No more digging through heavy books, and hoping that the right word is near enough to use in a sentence. This app provides a fully functioning voice search, word of the day delivery, a favorite words list and trending and popular words that others are looking up around you. With over 375,000 definitions, word origins and histories, as well as the proper way to use them in a sentence, each can be referenced in a matter of seconds. And when you simply cannot resist, share words with others through email, SMS, Facebook and Twitter.

Fandango Movies - Times & Tickets by Fandango, Inc.

Watch movie trailers, read reviews from fans and critics alike, and purchase your movie tickets directly from your Kindle with the Fandango app. Reserved seating is even available at select locations, so there's no need to hold seats or get to the theatre an hour early! Fandango allows you to create an account, which will store your credit card information for future purchases, so there is no need to grab your purse or wallet each time you want to buy tickets. Once you've viewed the picture, add your own feedback as a review for future viewers, or post your assessment of the movie, its characters and story line to your Facebook wall.

Banking (Credit Card) App

Finally, one of the best apps you can employ on your Nexus 7 is your banking app, which will give you at a glance account balances and the ability to transfer money, pay a bill or simply know what transactions have cleared and which ones are pending. Simply type in the name of your particular bank into the Google Play store to reveal the available apps for your device. Any banking app should be free, but it is important to ensure the app you choose is the one affiliated directly with your bank. It is probably smart to go to the bank's website on your device, and look for direct link to their app. This app idea also works with credit cards, so you know exactly what your balance is or what has been charged to your card in the last billing cycle. Apps provide the perfect escape from the online hustle and bustle, so use them to your advantage where you can!

10 Great Nexus 7 Games

Gaming may seem like something teenagers do, and if you are not one you may feel a little suspicious downloading them. Don't. Games are a great way to take your mind off the busy world for a while, and even an appropriate way to kill time between appointments. Games keep your mind active, and allow you to enjoy the graphics and sounds of your Google Nexus 7. Here are some of the great ones you may want to consider!

Candy Crush Saga

You know you love it, even if you have not had the opportunity to play it regularly! With hundreds of levels to conquer, there is seemingly no end to this precious entertainment app. The concept involves lining up candies to crush them and move through the various puzzles and levels. The game can be integrated with your Facebook, so that friends can provide you with extra lives, tools or moves, or you can choose to make an in-app purchase for these extras. Keep a close eye on your movements, however, because this game is addicting!

Dungeon Hunter 4

If you are in the mood to fight and plunder, while being immersed into a fully realized animated story, Dungeon Hunter 4 is for you! The game exists as a competitive, multiplayer platform that allows you to pit your characters against those of your rivals, as the action packed story plays out before your eyes. Downloading or playing the previous versions are not necessary to enjoy this gripping game. The app is also available for free, making it even better!

Triple Town

Triple Town is an addictive and appealing app that allows you to build a great city through the use of a puzzle game! Players accumulate points by building big cities – the bigger, the more points – and compete with other players internationally to see who is the best structural engineer who can match the most game pieces to bring their city to life! The app is free, and tournaments are available occasionally for players to go all in on the experience.

Words with Friends

Words with Friends has taken the app world by storm, and brought friends together from across the globe, while pitting their wordsmithing techniques against each other. The game operates similar to Scrabble in that you are given titles to create words with – piecing them together using the existing words on the board. In addition to a cool technological advancement in word games that this app employs, you can chat with the person you are playing against in a sidebar! You can have as many games as you can handle going at once, allowing you to play with your parents and your old college roommate in separate games without issue. The app keeps score for you, and even provides a history of your games won, lost and opponents. The app is free, as long as you do not mind advertisements popping up in between moves. You can pay for the professional version, and go ad free, for $4.99.

100 Floors

This creative app requires you to complete puzzles by moving blocks and bins or pushing buttons to unlock the doors to each level, and move onto the next floor. Although the app itself provides very little direction on how to proceed through each floor, the creativity and design is enough to keep you coming back for more in a quest to clear each level as efficiently as possible. You may be required to tap, pinch, poke, shake, tilt or expand the screen in order to pass the level you are on, so do not be afraid to get creative with the process!

Beastie Bay

This game by Kairosot Co., Ltd. was made available in 2013 and will give a visualizing arcade and action experience on your tablet. Your character washes ashore on an unknown island surrounded by savage beasts. The objectives are simple: survive, and if possible, thrive! The game is much like other titles where you are developing your skills and building up your civilization on this desolate island. Loads of fun, and full of great graphics, puzzles and rewards!

Can You Escape 2?

The sequel to the original "Can You Escape?" is just as fun and captivating! This game involves solving puzzles based on clues in a room to escape from the room. Find all of the hidden objects in the room required to get out of there and advance to the next level. It involves great graphics, challenging puzzles and increasing levels of difficulty to keep puzzle/strategy fans entertained for hours! Download this game by MobiGrow from Google Play and see how many levels you can defeat!

Gyro

This game by Vivid Games S.A. is an entertaining arcade and action title that will challenge some for hours, and drive others bonkers trying to win! The concept seems simple, you've got a multicolored wheel in the center of your screen. Different colored dots come flying at the wheel from all directions. Your goal? Twist and turn your tablet so that you have the dots going to the correct color on your wheel! Sounds simple, but after a while this one may test your patience! Great for endless entertainment, whether bored at home, or on a long flight somewhere!

Heroes of Order and Chaos

This is a Multiplayer Online Battle Arena (MOBA) strategy game in the style of "League of Legends." Gameloft has created this multiplayer online game with tons of free heroes to choose from and amazing gameplay. The experience includes building up a team (of other online friends or players), building up skills and destroying the enemy base. Heroes include melee bruisers, wizards, and more, with a rotation of free Heroes to choose from. The real-time action of this game will certainly draw in fans of this genre of game, and for free you can't beat the graphics and gameplay!

Real Soccer 2013

When it comes to free sports games, it's hard to rival Real Soccer 13 by Gameloft. The game's graphics and features are among the best for a free title which involves controlling, developing and bringing your club to the championship. It contains 700-motion capture animations and improved gameplay which is said to give a "TV-like experience" and amazing effects. Add this free sports simulation game to your tablet if you or someone who uses your Nexus 7 loves the game of soccer.

Nexus 7 Accessories

There are all sorts of different accessories that can accompany your Nexus 7, to ensure the proper care is used during its operation. Let's look at some of the ways to protect your device, extend its life and make it much more useful overall for your daily operations.

Case

Every tablet needs a case to ensure that it is not damaged during an inadvertent drop or equally chilling toss of a bag, briefcase or backpack. These can also help your tablet to stand out from the pack, giving it a colorful or more stylish look. Although there is a Google-branded case, it is important simply to find one that fits the Nexus 7 so that the fit is snug for safety. Leather, cloth, plastic and patterns of all kind are available at nearly any big box retailer. Some cases will also allow you to fold them in such a way that you can use them as a way to stand up your tablet for easier screen-viewing.

Stylus

If you prefer to use a Stylus pen, instead of your fingers, search for the latest technology that provides an ultra-sensitive tip so the application is effortless and responsive. It will simply need to be compatible to the Nexus 7, and can be purchased for under $10 at any electronic retailer in person or online. Sometimes these will be especially useful for drawing apps, writing apps or games.

Screen Protector

Screen protectors are incredibly important to your device's longevity, as they will protect the tablet from scratching or cracking, while minimizing fingerprints and glare along the way. There are many varieties available including those that help cut down on the glare factor when the sunlight hits your screen. Most screen protectors are sold in packs of at least three. There may also be kiosks and stores at your nearby mall that will help to install these, to make for a cleaner look, with less air bubbles.

External Power Chargers

If you use your device on the go, and never know when there is going to be an outlet available to recharge, consider purchasing an external power charger that operates as a high capacity, quick juice outlet without any electricity necessary. These chargers are small, portable and available in price ranges from $15 to $50 and allow you to simply plug your Google Nexus 7 in while you are camping or giving an impromptu presentation in a parking lot. Using your device is only possible if the battery is charged, and these external chargers will help ensure that is the case at all times, so you are never without your device. Some of the best external chargers are made by Halo and Anker, and can be purchased online at various websites.

WiFi Media Drives

Whether you are backing up your beloved photos and videos, or simply transferring music and movies to a location other than your Nexus 7, a WiFi media drive will help you store everything safely. The best part is, with the WiFi technology, you can wirelessly stream your media and files to your tablet on-the-go and off-the-grid. The WiFi also creates its own wireless network, so there is no need for you to find a Hotspot while you are traveling or in need of directions. You can also download the content from your media drive to your tablet, so you can enjoy where WiFi cannot be used including during flight. Prices vary incredibly for these devices, and it would simply take a closer look to determine which capacity you would need. One variety of this is the Sandisk Connect, which is currently sold in 32 and 64 gigabyte sizes and should work with your tablet.

Google Chromecast

One of the best bargains yet is the Google Chromecast, which has been selling for around $30 to $35 at various retailers. This device allows you to stream media from your Nexus 7 tablet to your television! This means you can watch movies, videos or even look at pictures with your friends and family without everyone crowding around your electronic device. Simply pick the media you would like to transfer, plug the Chromecast into your HDMI ready television, sync the two and stream away! You can watch your HBO Go, Netflix or Hulu Plus account, or listen to Pandora and watch YouTube videos on the big screen! There's more apps on the way, and the fact that both devices come from Google, makes them work together brilliantly.

Bluetooth Speakers & Headphones

Music and movies can be even more enjoyable on your device with the use of an external bluetooth wireless speaker, or a great pair of headphones. Some of the recommended brands of Bluetooth speaker include JBL, Sonos and Bose. There are cheaper alternatives as well, but one of my personal favorites is the JBL Flip, which generally sells for under $100 and produces amazing sound in a compact speaker.
As for headphones, there are plenty of options out there, depending on what you want to spend and what sort of headphones you want to use. Beats by Dre, Bose, and Sennheiser are a few personal favorites to check into to help really enjoy your music on another level! If you're a frequent traveler look for noise-cancelling headphones for long flights. You'll be glad you invested in them!

Docking Station from ASUS

ASUS has The Official Nexus 7 dock available, which is a convenient way to display your device, and allow its USB ports to be free in order to charge the device through special gold pins. With this device, you can stand your tablet up in landscape mode to enjoy movies, music, the internet or other options. You'll also be able to use the audio out in case you want to hook up your device to speakers or a headset. This docking stations generally costs about $40 or so at various retailers.

Conclusion

Mobile devices are quickly becoming the norm and the Google Nexus 7 is clearly one of the top choices for consumers to use. It allows for a wide variety of tasks, whether they are checking emails, watching videos or movies, streaming music, taking and storing photos, posting a social media status, or simply browsing the web. The Nexus 7 also has a brilliant screen, so no matter what you are doing you can enjoy the graphics, movies, and productions exactly as they were planned to be viewed by the creator. Games and news apps come to life, providing exceptional colors, brilliant contrast and amazing quality, all in a 7" screen.

Feel free to work from home on your device, or use it simply for entertainment purposes as both are equally accessible with a slide of your fingertips across the screen. Explore your device and all it has to offer by using the tips provided in this guide, and get the most out of your device no matter where you are, on the go or at home.

This versatile tablet provides amazing functionality in a small package, which means its transportability is unmatched. Enjoy everything it has to offer, and show your friends just how much you can do with this tablet now that you've gained a fuller understanding of all its amazing capabilities.

Resources

For all the resources mentioned in this book, please use your smartphone or tablet to scan the QR code provided below to get a list of the links online.

More Books by Shelby Johnson

iPad Mini User's Guide: Simple Tips and Tricks to Unleash the Power of your Tablet!
iPhone 5 (5C & 5S) User's Manual: Tips and Tricks to Unleash the Power of Your Smartphone! (includes iOS 7)
Kindle Fire HD User's Guide Book: Unleash the Power of Your Tablet!
Facebook for Beginners: Navigating the Social Network
Kindle Paperwhite User's Manual: Guide to Enjoying your E-reader!
How to Get Rid of Cable TV & Save Money: Watch Digital TV & Live Stream Online Media
Chromecast User Manual: Guide to Stream to Your TV (w/Extra Tips & Tricks!)